Introduction

Sometimes I feel like I don't know too much about this fashion industry
I'm in a rut
I want to be like Anna
But have swag like Donatella
I want to be featured
Snapped by the paparazzi
Everybody loves Givenchy
Balmain and Balenciaga
I'm still trying to save to get that Chanel from the nearest consignment
Designers started somewhere
And so did the stylists
I'm just trying to get to the point where I have my own stylist
And man I love writing
I think it'll make me rich
But it's only determined by you continuously giving my pages a flip.

RIDICULOUSLY FAVORED

I Wish My Name Was Fashion

I Wish My Name Was Fashion

So I could be like vogue, be detailed with fancy buttons, a pant with luxurious creases and folds.

I wish my name was fashion, photoshoots feature only me.

My parents would be haute couture; I would be fit for the queen.

I wouldn't have to the follow the rules; I would have a huge imagination.

I wish my name was Fashion.

Runway would be my destination.

I would be among the stars.

Purses, jewelry, sunglasses, every red carpet I would be a part of.

I wish my name was fashion.

With a nickname of Grace or Anna.

I would forecast the trends; I would be one big extravaganza.

I wish my name was fashion so I would never worry.

My mom would always get gifts leaving daddy's pockets sturdy.

I wish my name was fashion, last but not least.

Everyone would love me; I would always be the one to please.

I wish my name was fashion because one day it will be mine.

Whether I'm a star designer, editor, or icon, I will shine.

I wish my name was fashion, Paris, London, Tokyo, Milan, NYC.

So much passion, fun, and hard work would exult from within me.

I wish my name was fashion because it's something that I love.

If my name was fashion.... I would do more than just exist, I would create another world.

Grande

Fashion should be bigger

Where are our televised Oscar Awards?

Where are our families crowded at the TV to see what fashion wore?

Where are our astronaut trophies?

Our orange colored blimp?

I have yet to see a superstar wear a dress made out of gimp

I have yet to see an arena full of pretty little faces

Famous modeling troupes can perform

Famous supermodels can grace us

Fashion should be bigger

Stop the, stop the, press

Fashion should be bigger

Something more and nothing less

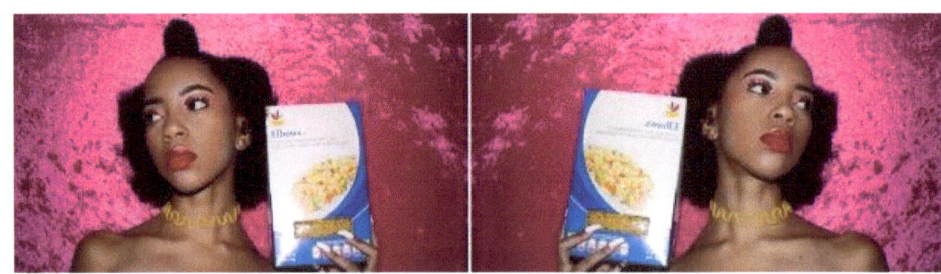

Boss

I want to model

I want to design

I want to create the fashion stories on a fashion magazines invisible lines

I don't care what it is or whatever it may be

As long as it allows me to be a boss in the fashion industry

A creative director, a creative VP

A style maven like Rihanna

Add icon please

Determine It All

Every time there is fashion week

I wish I was there

Oh how I love looking at models and their beautiful blank stares

Oh how I would love to sit front row with fashions top editor

Interviewers asking "Are you enjoying the show?"

Yes I am girl, you bet I am

This is the life to have first pick

This is the life to determine it all

You can decide what designer prevails or falls

Stylish Situation

If you can make it, you can wear it

Do you not see that you have them staring!

That is so cute love, look at you!

OMG where did you get those shoes?!

They are stylish, give us a twist!

Yes they are going on my shopping list!

And that bag, yes you are wearing it!

I have to get my own and I am not sharing it!

And those shades, they are blocking the sun!

Even the sun is asking where you got those from

And that outfit, to it I will salute

Denim on Denim will not ever get the boot!

Confessions of a Shopaholic

Five dollars or 200?

I'd wear it if it is fly

Five dollars or 200?

Either one would catch some eyes

When you are in a fashion dilemma, which one will be the winner?

Charge the card or spend the cash?

Charge it all or make it last?

Five dollars or 200?

If you love it, 200 is the smallest number

Schmood.

Who cannot wait until New York Nordies gets there plenty story following?

What about the first black editor in chief at Teen Vogue?

What if the next spotlighted designer doesn't sell?

Think of all of the fashion knowledge she must hold

What about the faces of our future?

Style starts with the different ways children learn to tie their shoestrings

It grows when he wants to wear a Batman cape to school

You know the way you dress is based off of your changing mood

Sometimes it is simply because it is the dress code on an invitation

It says to dress Hollywood but you want to dress with simplification

It can be a rainy day and the weather is just crap

But on this rainy day you feel super sexy, so it is heels over flats

Me

When someone says fashion, ask them do they know me.

Good Looking

High heels, flats, Tims, or butters

When it is cold I use my puffer coat to cover

Tons of lingerie is never a sin

I can't wait until it is hot to wear bikinis to swim

Chokers, necklaces, bracelets galore

You will never have enough of it

So you will always need more

Handbags, back packs, oh I need this clutch

If you get the designer mug

You will definitely need the designer thermal cup

Home decor with fashion

There is no limit

"I Love Fashion" sticker on my car window that is so fiercely tinted

Skinny jeans or jeans that plump the booty

Fashion has me looking good

I am the cutie on duty

Don't Give Up

Sewing machine, thread, I stuck myself with a needle

If I sew in the wrong spot this time I will quit and be a kindergarten teacher

I have to get it right

Because I know they will love my style

This is one trial in my many other trials

I will not give up, I just have to practice

I have to find a way to end this sticking myself with a sewing needle tragic

Now I'm bleeding

There is blood on my trim

It makes me want to give up and go buy the latest trend

...

Do not give up

Saturday Night

I must have those shoes

I hope they have my size

And I need a matching outfit

I could wear it Saturday night

And what about my hair

Cute clothes just won't do

Let me call my hairdresser

I need the hook up boo!

Bags, pearls, diamonds

Lipstick, blush, and gold chains

You're a newborn and I'm an adult when it comes to this fashion thing

Quote Me

Diagnosed with fashion. I'm not looking for a cure.

More

Much more than your average.

Way better than the ordinary.

Frog in Your Throat?

My Effect Is Everlasting.

Salad Dressing

Muse.Naked.

Socks. Naked.

Panties.Naked.

Bra.Naked.

Deodorant.Underwear.

Skirt.Heels.

Shirt was wrinkled. Iron. Ironing Board.Spray Perfume. Fix My Hair.

Bag.Check!

Car keys.

Check.

Coat... Maybe... Is it chilly where you are at?

Lipstick.Eyeshadow.

Full Face.Beat.

Earrings. Bracelets. Add some rings.

Call me salad. Continually dressing me.

Multiple flavors.

Everyday.

Fashion School

I remember those late nights at the 24 hour McDonalds after slaving in the 24 hour design lab.

Two Bros Pizza.

NYC.

If you know what I mean.

AlphaBETs

A is for A-Line

B is for body

C is for culotte

D is for Designer

E is for embroidery

F is for fit

G is for gimp

H is for hem

I is for instant style

J is for jerseys

K is for knickerbockers

L is for Laundry

M is for millinery

N is for non-woven

O is for oxford

P is for peplum that is soothing

Q is for quilted

R is for ruffles

S is for signature

T is for Tea party attire and chocolate truffles

U is for umbrella hat

V is for v-neck

W is for wedge heels

X is for XL Sweatshirts

Y is for yellow polka dot bikini

Z is for zebra print

Fashionably Late

If I change my bag, I have to change my shoes.

If I change my bottoms, the shirt goes too.

If my hair is not done, I'm not going.

If you tell me how to dress for it in advance, I MIGHT arrive early.

Yawning

I told my grandma that I've been yawning all day.

But she thought that I said yarning.

So she grabbed her bucket of yarn because she wanted to start yarning.

I finally had my chance to sleep but somebody rang my bell.

It was my grandma with her bucket of yarn ready to go to town.

Nothing to Wear

I always feel like I have nothing to wear

when my clothes in my closet don't represent the look I want to give.